# *Carols*
# BY CANDLELIGHT

Illustrated by Jane South

ERIC DOBBY PUBLISHING

# Contents

# While shepherds watched their flocks by night

While shepherds watched their
    flocks by night,
All seated on the ground,
The Angel of the Lord came down,
And glory shone around.

'Fear not,' said he (for mighty
    dread
Had seized their troubled mind),
'Glad tidings of great joy I bring
To you and all mankind.

'To you in David's town this day
Is born of David's line
A Saviour who is Christ the Lord –
And this shall be the sign:

'The heavenly Babe you there
     shall find
To human view displayed,
All meanly wrapped in
     swaddling bands,
And in a manger laid.'

Thus spake the Seraph, and
     forthwith
Appeared a shining throng
Of Angels, praising God, who thus
Addressed their joyful song:

'All glory be to God on high,
And to the earth be peace:
Goodwill henceforth from heaven
     to men
Begin and never cease.'

# Once in royal David's city

Once, in royal David's city,
    Stood a lowly cattle-shed,
Where a mother laid her baby,
    In a manger for His bed.
Mary was that mother mild,
    Jesus Christ her little child.

He came down to earth from heaven,
    Who is God and Lord of all,
And His shelter was a stable,
    And His cradle was a stall:
With the poor and mean and lowly
    Lived on earth our Saviour holy.

And through all His wondrous childhood
    He would honour and obey,
Love and watch the lowly mother,
    In whose gentle arms He lay.
Christian children all must be
    Mild, obedient, good as He.

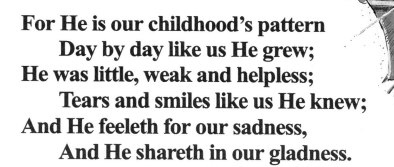

For He is our childhood's pattern
    Day by day like us He grew;
He was little, weak and helpless;
    Tears and smiles like us He knew;
And He feeleth for our sadness,
    And He shareth in our gladness.

And our eyes at last shall see Him,
    Through His own redeeming love;
For that child, so dear and gentle,
    Is our Lord in heaven above;
And He leads His children on
    To the place where He is gone.

Not in that poor lowly stable,
    With the oxen standing by,
We shall see Him; but in heaven,
    Set at God's right hand on high;
When like stars His children crowned,
    All in white shall wait around.

# O little town of Bethlehem

O little town of Bethlehem,
How still we see thee lie!
Above thy deep and dreamless sleep
The silent stars go by;
Yet in thy dark streets shineth
The everlasting Light;
The hopes and fears of all the years
Are met in thee to-night.

O morning stars, together
Proclaim the holy birth,
And praises sing to God the King,
And peace to men on earth;
For Christ is born of Mary;
And, gathered all above,
While mortals sleep, the Angels keep
Their watch of wondering love.

How silently, how silently,
The wondrous gift is given!
So God imparts to human hearts
The blessings of His heaven,
No ear may hear His coming;
But in this world of sin,
Where meek souls will receive
    Him still
The dear Christ enters in.

O Holy Child of Bethlehem,
Descend to us, we pray;
Cast out our sin, and enter in;
Be born in us to-day.
We hear the Christmas Angels
The great glad tidings tell;
O come to us, abide with us,
Our Lord Emmanuel.

# As with gladness men of old

As with gladness men of old
Did the guiding star behold;
As with joy they hailed it's light,
Leading onward, beaming bright,
So, most gracious God, may we
Evermore be led to Thee.

As with joyful steps they sped,
Saviour, to Thy lowly bed,
There to bend the knee before
Him whom heaven and earth adore,
So may we with willing feet
Ever seek Thy mercy-seat.

As they offered gifts most rare
At Thy cradle rude and bare,
So may we with holy joy,
Pure, and free from sin's alloy,
All our costliest treasures bring,
Christ, to Thee, our Heavenly King.

Holy Jesus, every day
Keep us in the narrow way;
And, when earthly things are past,
Bring our ransomed souls at last
Where they need no star to guide,
Where no clouds Thy glory hide.

In the heavenly country bright
Need they no created light;
Thou its Light, its Joy, its Crown,
Thou its Sun, which goes not down.
There for ever may we sing
Hallelujahs to our King.

# *H*ark! the herald-angels sing

Hark! the herald-angels sing
Glory to the new-born King,
Peace on earth and mercy mild,
God and sinners reconciled.
Joyful, all ye nations, rise,
Join the triumph of the skies;
With the Angelic host proclaim,
Christ is born in Bethlehem.
   *Hark! the herald-angels sing*
   *Glory to the new-born King.*

Christ, by highest heaven adored,
Christ, the everlasting Lord,
Late in time behold Him come,
Offspring of a Virgin's womb!
Veiled in flesh the Godhead see!
Hail the Incarnate Deity!
Pleased as Man with man to dwell,
Jesus, our Emmanuel!
   *Hark! the herald-angels sing*

**Hail the Heaven-born Prince of Peace!**
**Hail the Sun of Righteousness!**
**Light and life to all He brings,**
**Risen with healing in His wings.**
**Mild, He lays His glory by,**
**Born that man no more may die,**
**Born to raise the sons of earth,**
**Born to give them second birth.**
   *Hark! the herald-angels sing*

# Good Christian men, rejoice

Good Christian men, rejoice
With heart, and soul, and voice;
Give ye heed to what we say:
News! News!
Jesus Christ is born to-day!
Ox and ass before Him bow,
And He is in the manger now.
*Christ is born to-day!*
*Christ is born to-day!*

Good Christian men, rejoice
With heart, and soul, and voice;
Now ye hear of endless bliss:
Joy! Joy!
Jesus Christ was born for this!
He hath ope'd the heavenly door
And man is blessed for evermore.
*Christ was born for this!*
*Christ was born for this!*

**Good Christian men rejoice
With heart, and soul, and voice;
Now ye need not fear the grave:
Peace! Peace!
Jesus Christ was born to save!
Calls you one and calls you all,
To gain His everlasting hall.**
   *Christ was born to save!*
   *Christ was born to save!*

# O come all ye faithful

O come all ye faithful,
Joyful and triumphant,
O come ye, O come ye
 to Bethlehem;
Come and behold Him,
Born the King of Angels:
 *O come, let us adore Him,*
 *O come, let us adore Him,*
 *O come, let us adore Him,*
 *Christ the Lord!*

God of God,
Light of light,
Lo! He abhors not the Virgin's
 womb;
Very God,
Begotten, not created:
 *O come, let us adore Him,*

Sing, choirs of Angels,
Sing in exultation,
Sing, all ye citizens of Heaven
    above:
'Glory to God
In the highest':
  *O come, let us adore Him,*

Yea, Lord we greet Thee,
Born this happy morning:
Jesus, to Thee be glory given,
Word of the Father,
Now in flesh appearing:
  *O come, let us adore Him,*

# The first Nowell the Angel did say

The first Nowell the Angel did say
Was to certain poor shepherds in
    fields as they lay;
In fields where they lay a-keeping
    their sheep,
On a cold winter's night that was so
    deep.
  *Nowell, Nowell, Nowell, Nowell,*
  *Born is the King of Israel!*

They looked up and saw a star
As it shone in the East, beyond them
    far;
And to the earth it gave great light,
And so it continued both day and
    night.
  *Nowell, Nowell, Nowell, Nowell,*
  *Born is the King of Israel!*

And by the light of that same star,
Three Wise Men came from country
    far:
To seek for a King was their intent,
And to follow the star wherever it
    went.
   *Nowell, Nowell, Nowell, Nowell,*
   *Born is the King of Israel!*

This star drew nigh to the north-
    west;
O'er Bethlehem it took its rest,
And there it did both stop and stay,
Right over the place where Jesus lay.
   *Nowell, Nowell, Nowell, Nowell,*
   *Born is the King of Israel!*

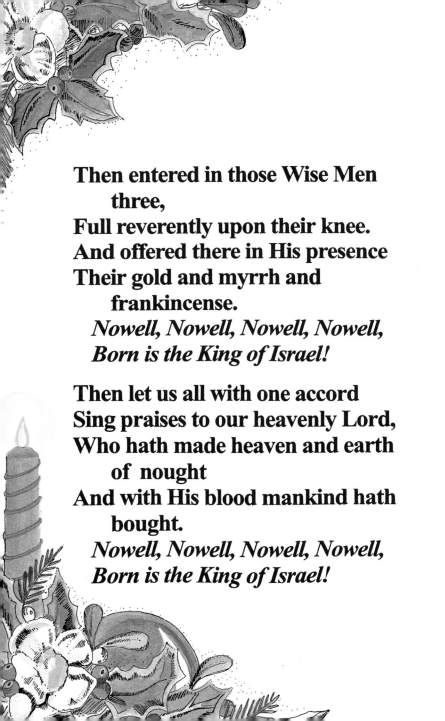

Then entered in those Wise Men three,
Full reverently upon their knee.
And offered there in His presence
Their gold and myrrh and frankincense.
*Nowell, Nowell, Nowell, Nowell,*
*Born is the King of Israel!*

Then let us all with one accord
Sing praises to our heavenly Lord,
Who hath made heaven and earth of nought
And with His blood mankind hath bought.
*Nowell, Nowell, Nowell, Nowell,*
*Born is the King of Israel!*

# _Still the night, holy the night_

Still the night, holy the night!
Sleeps the world; hid from sight,
Mary and Joseph in stable bare
Watch o'er the Child belovèd and fair,
    Sleeping in heavenly rest.

Still the night, holy the night!
Shepherds first saw the light,
Heard resounding clear and long,
Far and near, the angel-song,
    Christ the Redeemer is here!

Still the night, holy the night!
Son of God, O how bright
Love is shining from Thy face!
Strikes for us now the hour of grace,
    Saviour, since Thou art born!

# _Away in a manger, no crib for a bed_

Away in a manger, no crib for a bed,
The little Lord Jesus laid down His
    sweet head.
The stars in the bright sky looked
    down where He lay
The little Lord Jesus asleep on the
    hay.

The cattle are lowing, the Baby
    awakes,
But little Lord Jesus, no crying He
    makes,
I love Thee, Lord Jesus! look down
    from the sky,
And stay by my side until morning
    is nigh.

Be near me, Lord Jesus; I ask Thee
to stay
Close by me for ever, and love me, I
pray,
Bless all the dear children in Thy
tender care,
And fit us for heaven to live with
Thee there.

# Angels from the realms of glory

Angels from the realms of glory,
Wing your flight o'er all the earth,
Ye who sang creation's story
Now proclaim Messiah's birth:
*Come ... and worship*
*Worship Christ the King*
*Come ... and worship*
*Worship Christ, the new-born King.*

Shepherds in the fields abiding,
Watching o'er your flocks by night,
God with man is now residing;
Yonder shines the infant Light:
*Come ... and worship*
*Worship Christ the King*
*Come ... and worship*
*Worship Christ, the new-born King.*

Sages, leave your contemplations,
Brighter visions beam afar;
Seek the great Desire of nations;
Ye have seen His natal star:
  *Come ... and worship*
  *Worship Christ the King*
  *Come ... and worship*
  *Worship Christ, the new-born King.*

Saints before the alter bending,
Watching long in hope and fear,
Suddenly the Lord, descending,
In His temple shall appear:
  *Come ... and worship*
  *Worship Christ the King*
  *Come ... and worship*
  *Worship Christ, the new-born King.*

# See, amid the winter's snow

See, amid the winter's snow,
Born for us on earth below,
See, the tender Lamb appears,
Promised from eternal years.
*Hail, Thou ever-blessed morn!*
*Hail, Redemption's happy dawn!*
*Sing through all Jerusalem,*
*Christ is born in Bethlehem.*

Lo, within a manger lies
He who built the starry skies;
He who, throned in height sublime,
Sits amid the Cherubim!
*Hail, Thou ever-blessed morn!*

Say, ye holy shepherds, say,
What your joyful news to-day;
Wherefore have ye left your sheep
On the lonely mountain steep?
*Hail, Thou ever-blessed morn!*

As we watched at dead of night,
Lo, we saw a wondrous light;
Angels singing Peace on earth
Told us of a Saviour's Birth.
   *Hail, Thou ever-blessed morn!*

Sacred Infant, all divine,
What a tender love was Thine,
Thus to come from highest bliss
Down to such a world as this!
   *Hail, Thou ever-blessed morn!*

Teach, O teach us, Holy Child,
By Thy face so meek and mild,
Teach us to resemble Thee,
In Thy sweet humility.
   *Hail, Thou ever-blessed morn!*

# *I saw three ships come sailing in*

I saw three ships come sailing in,
  *On Christmas Day, On Christmas
  Day;*
I saw three ships come sailing in,
  *On Christmas Day in the morning.*

And what was in those ships all three?

The Virgin Mary and Christ were
  there

Pray, whither sailed those ships all
  three?

O, they sailed into Bethlehem.

And all the bells on earth shall ring.

And all the Angels in Heaven shall
  sing.

And all the souls on earth shall sing.

Then let us rejoice again!

# Ding dong! merrily on high

Ding dong! merrily on high
    in heaven the bells are ringing;
Ding dong! verily the sky
    is riv'n with angels singing:
    *Gloria, Hosanna in excelsis.*

E'en so here below, below,
    let steeple bells be swungen,
And i-o, i-o, i-o by priest
    and people sungen!
    *Gloria, Hosanna in excelsis.*

Pray you, dutifully prime
    your matin chime, ye ringers;
May you beautifully rime
    your eve-time song, ye singers:
    *Gloria, Hosanna in excelsis.*

# *We three kings of Orient are*

We three kings of Orient are;
Bearing gifts we traverse afar
Field and fountain, moor and
     mountain,
Following yonder star:
*O star of wonder, star of night,*
*Star with royal beauty bright,*
*Westward leading, still proceeding,*
*Guide us to Thy perfect light.*

Melchior:
Born a King on Bethlehem plain,
Gold I bring to crown Him again –
King forever, ceasing never,
Over us all to reign:
*O star of wonder, star of night,*
*Star with royal beauty bright,*
*Westward leading, still proceeding,*
*Guide us to Thy perfect light.*

**Gaspar:**
**Frankincense to offer have I;**
**Incense owns a Deity nigh:**
**Prayer and praising, all men raising,**
**Worship Him, God most high:**
    *O star of wonder, star of night,*
    *Star with royal beauty bright,*
    *Westward leading, still proceeding,*
    *Guide us to Thy perfect light.*

**Balthazar:**
**Myrrh is mine; it's bitter perfume**
**Breathes a life of gathering gloom;**
**Sorrowing, sighing, bleeding, dying,**
**Sealed in a stone-cold tomb:**
    *O star of wonder, star of night,*
    *Star with royal beauty bright,*
    *Westward leading, still proceeding,*
    *Guide us to Thy perfect light.*

**All:**
**Glorious now, behold Him arise,**
**King, and God, and sacrifice**
**Heaven sings alleluya,**
**Alleluya the earth replies:**
*O star of wonder, star of night,*
*Star with royal beauty bright,*
*Westward leading, still proceeding,*
*Guide us to Thy perfect light.*